THE SUPERNATURAL

BY

RHIANNON LASSITER

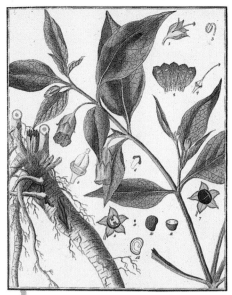

BLACK HATS & BROOMSTICKS

Women thought to have magic po[wers]
are called witches. In stories witc[hes]
wear black, ride broomsticks, and br[ew]
magic potions in black pots called
cauldrons. They also have *familiars* (spir[it]
helpers), often in the form of cats. If any
of this were true, witches would be very
easy to spot. In the past, many people
thought women were witches just
because they lived alone or
used herbs to cure illnesses.
Many characters in fairy tales
and other stories were based
on these old superstitions.
There are witches in
Shakespeare's
play *Macbeth*.

DEADLY NIGHTSHADE

Some plants, when
eaten or smoked, can
cause people to feel
strange or see frightening
things that are not real.
Belladonna (deadly
nightshade) is a poisonous plant. It was often used in magical
ceremonies. It can cause someone to feel like they're flying. This
hallucination (vision of something that is not really there) may be why
some people believed they were witches and confessed to
having flown by magical means.

🧠 FOOD FOR THOUGHT

The author Arthur C. Clarke wrote, "Any sufficiently advanced technology is indistinguishable from magic." Many of the things we take for granted—like radio, computers, and airplanes—would have seemed magical to our ancestors. It is human nature to look for explanations for what we do not understand. "Magic" can be used to explain almost anything! It may be that there are new sciences that we do not know about yet. Those unknown sciences could explain some of the things that seem like magic. And perhaps we like the idea of magic because we have no explanation for it?

THE COURT MAGICIAN

The English scholar Dr.
John Dee (1527–1608)
studied math, *astrology* (telling
fortunes based on the stars), and magic.
He practiced as a magician at European
courts. He claimed angels had taught him magic
spells. Queen Elizabeth I chose January 14 for her coronation (when she took the
throne) because Dr. Dee told her that date was good luck. A black crystal, which
he said had been given to him by an angel, can still be seen at the British Museum.

WITCHES & WARLOCKS

Events and our sense of things sometimes seem beyond understanding. Humankind has tended to use the existence of psychic abilities or supernatural powers to explain strange events. Religions, superstitions, and mysteries can rely on such beliefs. All through the twentieth century scientists have looked for explanations for a variety of strange *phenomena* (events). There remains much to discover and to understand. To unravel their mysteries we must first explore the history of beliefs in the *paranormal*, or unearthly.

MAGIC OF THE GODS

The priests and priestesses of ancient religions used magical rituals in their ceremonies. Gods like the Egyptian Isis (*above*) and the Persian Mithras had secrets. Only their followers were allowed to know these mysteries. Becoming one with the god was the main goal of the rituals. Isis was a goddess of love, death, cunning, and magic. Magical writing and picture writing called hieroglyphs were written in her temples. Because Isis means wisdom, her followers were expected to be intelligent and reasoning. Plutarch, an ancient Greek philosopher, described Isis worshippers as seekers of the hidden truths behind the gods.

A DEMONIC PACT

Witches and warlocks were suspected of working with the Devil. The Devil gave them magical powers in return for their souls. Anyone who claimed they could do magic was therefore believed to be unholy. The English playwright Christopher Marlowe (1564–93) and the German poet Johann Wolfgang von Goethe (1749–1832) both wrote plays about Georg Faust (1480–1538). Dr. Faust was a legendary German magician who sold his soul in return for knowledge. He is shown here standing within the protection of a ritual circle. He is summoning Mephistopheles, an agent of the Devil.

KEEPING EVIL AWAY

Many customs and superstitions are based on magic. Most of them are designed to keep evil away. There are also certain items that are believed to have magic powers. For example, a horseshoe hung over a doorway is thought to prevent witches from entering.

BLACK & WHITE MAGIC

The practice of magic is often separated into two categories. Black magic includes magic rites that make use of blood, death, and the name of the Devil. White magic includes powers of healing, visions, and some religious ceremonies. Some people practice magic today, but mostly without the rituals used in the past. Not all people who practice magic think of themselves as either black or white magicians. Some think the study of magic is a scienc They believe it can be used for either good or evil purposes. Others choos to study only white or only black magic.

FOOD FOR THOUGHT

Witchcraft used to be an easy excuse for bad luck. If a cow got sick or crops didn't grow, it was easier to blame an old woman who lived alone than to accept that you had been unlucky. Fear of witchcraft spread quickly. Anyone who did not join in blaming witches for unlucky events might have been accused of being a witch themselves. This led to many witch trials. Famous witch trials happened in Salem, Massachusetts, in 1692. In Salem, more than 150 people were arrested for witchcraft during the panic. In seventeenth-century Europe, even a birthmark could make people believe you were a witch. As many as 40,000 people were executed in Britain alone—even more were killed in Europe as a whole.

CRYSTAL HEALING

It is a long-held belief that crystals and some gems have magic healing properties. In Egypt, magicians sometimes told people to eat the powdered remains of magical jewelry or crystals to cure illness. This belief is still popular today. Crystal healers claim they can cure minor illnesses. Some even say that crystals help heal more dangerous diseases. Usually, a crystal is simply placed against the skin of a patient. Sometimes it is crushed and eaten.

DEVIL WORSHIP

Witches and black magicians who made deals with the Devil held ceremonies to worship him. The Black Mass was based on Christian worship, but designed to summon the Devil instead. It often involved acts of evil designed to please the Devil. The Witches' Sabbat was a midnight ritual in which witches and demons danced around a fire. The tradition is probably connected to older Celtic festivals held on May Day and Halloween. The Witches' Sabbat is still held today, but it is not necessarily used to summon the Devil. It can also be held as a celebration of birth and new life.

SOLOMON THE MAGICIAN

King Solomon of Israel, who lived in the tenth century BCE, was said to be a great magician. *The Key of Solomon*, one of the oldest known books of spells, tells how he captured evil spirits in a glass bottle. The book was used by black magicians because it also told how to make a deal with the Devil. They wanted the Devil's help to get rich and live longer. Solomon's Seal (two interlocked triangles) is often used in magic rites.

VOODOO

Voodoo is a religious cult practiced in parts of Africa, South America, and the Caribbean. It comes from a combination of Catholicism and West African traditions. Voodoo followers believe that a person in a trance can be possessed by their ancestors or gods. This is good for the person in this religion. However, voodoo also has a dark side when used in black magic. Voodoo sorcerers claim they can create *zombies*—people raised from the dead—who must obey the sorcerer's commands. Voodoo dolls are made by sorcerers using hair or nail clippings of a living person. Sticking pins into the doll is believed to harm the person it represents.

5

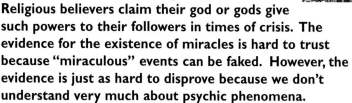

FOOD FOR THOUGHT

Belief in miracles is common to all religions. It suggests a basic human desire to trust in a higher power. We know that strong faith can allow people to do things they normally are not able to do. Studies of religious leaders called fakirs have shown that training and faith allow the human mind and body to perform amazing feats. Research suggests that self-hypnotism and excellent muscle control could be responsible for the ability of fakirs. It could mean that we are all able to perform amazing psychic feats. Fakirs actually do because of self-belief.

MYSTICISM & MIRACLES

The psychic powers of prophets and mystics may be believed by their religious followers, but their existence has not been proven scientifically. Every major religion has stories of miracles performed by priests and saints who possessed unusual and powerful abilities. Religious believers claim their god or gods give such powers to their followers in times of crisis. The evidence for the existence of miracles is hard to trust because "miraculous" events can be faked. However, the evidence is just as hard to disprove because we don't understand very much about psychic phenomena.

THE SHROUD OF TURIN

First displayed in 1353, the Shroud of Turin has the image of a crucified man on it. It was said to be the burial sheet of Jesus Christ. In 1989, carbon-dating methods were used to find how old it is. The results suggested the shroud was made between 1260 and 1390. This is many centuries later than Christ's death. However, there have been claims that scientists who wanted to disprove Christianity faked the carbon-dating tests. Some still believe the shroud is a holy relic.

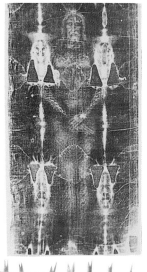

STIGMATA

Stigmata are the five wounds left on Christ after he was nailed to the cross. Since the crucifixion similar wounds have appeared on certain people, such as Antonio Ruffini (*right*). The people who get the stigmata are generally Christians with strong beliefs. Their religious beliefs may be all that they have in common. Stigmata do not seem to be caused by disease or injury. Some people's wounds last for years. Others heal quickly. Today, stigmata remain a scientific mystery. They are considered by the Roman Catholic Church to be a miracle.

HEALING POWERS

Certain religious statues and paintings are believed to have miraculous powers. Some people believe that these objects can heal minor and even deadly illnesses. Every year, thousands of people make long journeys called *pilgrimages* to religious sites. For many of them it is their last hope of becoming well. These "cures" often have an immediate positive effect but there is still no proof that they make long-term improvements to health. One statue said to have the power to heal is the Madonna at Lourdes in France (*left*).

THE RESURRECTION OF CHRIST

Resurrection, or returning to life after death, is part of many religions. It is one of the most impressive kinds of miracles. There are many skeptics who don't believe in divine miracles like resurrection. They sometimes claim that the prophets and demi-gods of ancient religions were actually people with powerful psychic powers.

FAKIRS

Indian fakirs enter a trance-like state in order to perform amazing acts of endurance. In 1835, the Maharaja of Lahore asked a fakir named Haridas to demonstrate his abilities. Haridas was buried underground in a locked coffin. Barley was planted in the earth above the coffin. Forty days later Haridas was dug out of the ground. He was alive and well. He was never found to have cheated. Fakirs still give displays of their powers. These powers include lying unhurt on a bed of nails, walking on hot coals, and floating above the ground. Although these psychic phenomena have been witnessed and recorded, scientists are still trying to figure out how some of them are done.

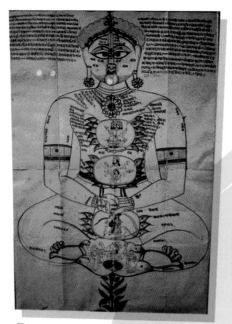

MAGIC ENERGIES, PSYCHIC POWERS

Different belief systems have developed around supernatural powers. Some of these beliefs involve worship. The people who hold these beliefs think of psychic phenomena as a form of religious activity. Some people believe *paranormal* (unexplained, sometimes ghostly) powers are part of normal life and try to live according to detailed rituals. Others fear any experience of the supernatural and try to completely ignore it. Our interest in the paranormal will keep people studying and trying to understand supernatural abilities and events that do not fit existing ideas about the world.

CHAKRA POINTS

Chakra is the Hindu word to describe the main centers of spiritual power in the human body. These are points along the spine where some people believe energy is changed into a usable form. Raw energy is said to be taken from the Earth and fed into the chakra points. There are seven principle chakras in the body. Detailed maps of the chakras and their connecting lines are used in some Eastern religions. They have also been used in Eastern medicine for thousands of years.

LEGENDARY TREASURES

Ancient pagans believed in the balance of the elements (earth, fire, air, and water). They also believed in four legendary items of great power. In mythology, these treasures are usually a sword, a spear, a cup, and a stone. Each has different powers and stories attached to it. Pagan legends tell of the Cauldron of Dagda, a cup of plenty said to provide a never-ending supply of food. The four objects are also symbols in the *Tarot*, a deck of cards used in fortune-telling. Magical items appear throughout history. During World War II Adolf Hitler collected such objects. He believed that he could not be defeated if he had them.

RITUAL PAINTINGS

The life of the Navajo Indians, who live in Arizona and New Mexico, include rituals and magical rites. The Navajo take good care of the environment. They carry out their daily activities with customs and chants intended to bri good fortune and to keep away evil. One of their most interesting rituals is the curing ceremony. A *medicine man* (a sorcerer who tends the spiritual well-being o tribe) conducts the ceremony. It involves drawing paintings in sand. The Navajo believe this activity helps to cure illness. Rather than magic, perhaps such rituals help to focus the mind. Believing they'll work may be enoug to make them work.

CHI ENERGY

The Chinese discipline of chi is used in acupuncture (an Eastern form of healing) and in the martial art t'ai chi ch'uan. Chi is the energy in all living things. This belief is also part of other cultures and religions. The yin-yang in Taoism symbolizes the two main forces of energy that are opposite and yet also work together. Yin is female and negatively charged. Yang is male and positively charged. Each contains part of the other, as seen in the yin-yang symbol at the center of this picture of three t'ai chi wise men. A master of chi can give an object more chi. In a surprising move, the Sony Corporation paid for a seven-year project into psychic phenomena. These tests included one in which a person who practiced chi tried to project chi energy into one of two glasses of water. A second person who practiced chi then tried to choose the glass with more chi energy. These tests reported a 70 percent success rate. However, the test conditions and controls have not been checked out.

FOOD FOR THOUGHT

Well-established magical systems, such as chi, can be as clearly thought out and reliable as scientific knowledge. In China, for example, acupuncture, a treatment based on the chi system, has been accepted by science for hundreds of years. However, it took a long time for Western doctors to accept it as a medical treatment.

BLOOD MAGIC

One belief shared by different kinds of magicians is about the power of blood. Black magic ceremonies, voodoo, and African shamanism all include rituals that involve sacrificing animals. The animal sacrificed is usually a goat, but other animals may also be used.

MADMAN OR MAGICIAN?

Grigori Rasputin (c.1871–1916) was a Siberian monk whose bad reputation made the field of psychic research unpopular in Russia for many years. He gained a great deal of power at the court of Nicholas II, the last czar of Russia (1894–1917). Rasputin claimed his supernatural powers could cure Alexei, the czar's only son, of a blood disease. He convinced the czarina of his abilities. Her support of Rasputin hurt the royal family's reputation. Rasputin was eventually killed by nobles jealous of his influence.

GRAND MASTER OF THE GOLDEN DAWN

Aleister Crowley (1875–1947) wanted to be known as "the wickedest man alive." He became Grand Master of the Golden Dawn, a secret magic society, but was kicked out for extreme practices. He believed he was a vampire and tried many different things to improve his magical powers. He attracted many followers during and after his lifetime. He once said, "I may be a black magician but I'm a bloody great one."

CONJURING TRICKS

Harry Houdini was an *escapologist* (an expert in escaping) and *conjurer* (magician) who faked psychic abilities on stage. He was interested in spiritualism and published a book called *A Magician Among the Spirits*. He wanted his book to show that mediums, who say they talk to the dead, are fake. Because Houdini knew how to fake psychic powers he didn't believe they actually existed.

CONJURERS OR MAGICIANS?

Paranormal events and psychic powers are often faked by conjurers. These people develop methods to entertain or fool their audiences. Some stage magicians freely admit that their acts, such as mind-reading and floating, are tricks. Others claim their abilities are real. Magicians such as Aleister Crowley and Grigori Rasputin convinced themselves and other people that their psychic talents were real. But it is hard to believe their claims because being known as magicians brought them lots of money and power.

WHEN SCHOLARS KNOW SIN • JR. SKEPTIC • PSYCHOTHERAPY SNAKE OIL

SKEPTIC

Extraordinary Claims, Revolutionary Ideas & The Promotion of Science   Vol. 6 No. 3, 1998 $5.95 USA ($7.95 Can./Int'l)

NORM LEVITT ON WHY PROFESSORS BELIEVE WEIRD THINGS

SPECIAL SECTION: • NORM LEVITT ON SEX, RACE, & THE TRIALS OF THE NEW LEFT • WHEN SCHOLARS KNOW SIN— ALTERNATIVE RELIGIONS AND THEIR ACADEMIC SUPPORTERS • PSYCHOTHERAPY—THE SNAKE OIL OF THE 90S? • • MEMES—WHAT ARE THEY GOOD FOR? • FACILITATED COMMUNICATION: EIGHT YEARS AND COUNTING •
ALSO: • AN INTERVIEW WITH SKEPTICAL PARAPSYCHOLOGIST SUSAN BLACKMORE • FOUR DAYS ON PLANET RANDI • WACO DEBATE • IS GOD DEAD?—WHY NIETZSCHE AND TIME MAGAZINE WERE WRONG BY MICHAEL SHERMER • THE TRUE BELIEVERS BY JAMES RANDI • THE CASE FOR YODA • THE GRADUATE RECORD EXAM REEXAMINED • DUMBTH NEWS •
JR. SKEPTIC: • BIGFOOT! • CRYSTALS—EXPLORING THE REAL MAGIC • TESTING A DOWSING ROD •

PROFESSIONAL SKEPTICS

A *skeptic* is someone who doubts and questions accepted beliefs. They do not trust new theories and ideas until they are scientifically proven. Even when given proof they may not be convinced. *Skeptic* magazine tries to argue against beliefs that, in its opinion, are "180 degrees out of phase with reason."

THE POWER OF THE MIND

Uri Geller is a stage magician who claims to use the power of his mind to bend metal objects, restart watches, and force computers to break down. He has performed these acts and others under strict test conditions. He has also been called a fake by some. Since Uri Geller started out as a conjurer, people tend to doubt his psychic abilities. The phenomenon of metal-bending is not unique to Geller. It has been studied in others who claim to have a similar power. It has also been done by people who are experts in metals.

FOOD FOR THOUGHT

It is impossible to prove that a conjurer does not have magical powers. It may be possible to get the same results by non-magical means. That is not the same as proving the powers do not exist. Not many people really believe stage magicians have magical powers, but it is more fun to sit back and enjoy the show. The way some conjuring tricks are done—floating or making a railroad car disappear—might even be more impressive than if magic were actually being used.

SPIRITS & SPIRITUALISM

People who claim to have psychic abilities of
believe in *spirits*—non-physical beings who a
thought to be gods or the souls of
the dead. Some people claim they
can talk to spirits using psychic
powers. Spirits can be helpful,
guiding or teaching the humans
they care about. But some spirits
are believed to return to the physical
world to cause harm. Some spirits
are tricksters. These spirits,
amused by humans, play jokes on
people who attempt to talk to
them. Even among people who
believe spirits exist, there is
no dependable theory about
what they are. People also
disagree about what
methods should be used to
talk with them.

SPIRIT GUIDES

Shamans, like other kinds of magicians, use spirit guides
as helpers and symbols in their magic. Brazilian shamans
believe people have spirits shaped like different animals.
The most powerful of these is the jaguar. Native
American shamanism involves adjusting magic to the path
of a different animal. A wolf shaman is expected to be
tireless and fierce. A coyote shaman plays tricks. Spirit
guides are not always animals. In shamanic magic, strong
images and physical symbols are important. The greater
the belief in a symbol, the greater its power.

REINCARNATION

Many people believe that after death a
person's soul is *reincarnated* (reborn)
in another body. Buddhists believe
that good or evil deeds in one life
will be rewarded or punished in
the next. Hindus believe a human
who leads an evil life may be
reincarnated as an animal. Those
who lead good lives move to ever-higher
levels of understanding in each life.
Finally they pass on to the next
stage of existence. Some
hypnotists have put people into
a trance-like state in which they
remember events that seem to
be from their previous lives. Some
people have even spoken in languages
they do not know in their present
life. However, it is difficult to prove
or disprove reincarnation.

 **FOOD FOR
THOUGHT**

*Belief that the soul or spirit
lives after death is common
throughout human history.
It hard to believe that
people just stop existing
when their bodies die. And if
people have spirits that are
not part of their bodies,
why shouldn't other
living things have
spirits as well?*

BODY AND SOUL

The ancient Egyptians believed that a person is divided into many different spiritual parts. Egyptian myths tell of great magicians who could separate their *ka* (soul or spirit double) from their body. The ka could fly in the form of a bird. Spells played an important part in the everyday lives of the Egyptians. They believed that all words have power, and they used them to make good things happen or to curse their enemies.

DREAMTIME

Aboriginal Australians have a rich set of beliefs about the supernatural powers of their ancestors. They call the time when the ancestors created everything that now exists Dreamtime. As shown in their rock paintings and artifacts, they see the natural world as a powerful and mysterious place. They do not separate the commonplace and the supernatural. They think both are important parts of life.

SHAMANISM AND WITCH DOCTORS

Today, there are shamans in Africa, South America, and the Far East. In the United States, shamans still practice among some Native Americans. The shaman in this picture is from Nigeria in Africa. A tribal *shaman* (witch doctor) is a magician and healer who cares for the body and soul of his people. He performs many different tasks. He might be asked to hunt for a soul that was stolen by an enemy. He may also be called to cure an illness. Shamanism is often passed on through families of witches. After their deaths, they are believed to continue as guardian spirits of their tribe.

ECTOPLASM

This medium is producing *ectoplasm*. Ectoplasm is a substance that comes from the medium's body. Mediums say it gives a spirit physical form. Silvery-white in color, it looks like thin fabric and forms the body and clothes of a spirit while it is speaking. Touching a spirit formed of ectoplasm is said to make the medium ill. Although nobody has proven that ectoplasm is fake, it is possible to swallow cotton and gradually spit it out of your mouth.

REST IN PEACE?

The words "Rest in Peace" carved on gravestones seem to mean that the dead might not rest or be at peace. Over the centuries, many stories have been told about ghosts who do not rest. They haunt people or places for revenge or because they have left something undone in their lives. Some people have said that they live comfortably with supernatural neighbors. Others say ghosts are dangerous and can smash objects, make scary noises, and create a threatening feeling in a house.

CLAIRVOYANTS & MEDIUMS

Clairvoyancy, or talking to spirits, is one of the earliest recorded psychic phenomena. It is also one of the most profitable for tricksters. Clairvoyants and mediums claim that we can contact the spirit of a dead person through them. Some mediums only claim to be able to speak with these spirits. Others claim they can give them a physical form. Mediums have often been exposed as frauds or have admitted to lying to their clients. A grieving person's strong wish to contact a dead person they love makes them want to believe in such tricks. Although many mediums have claimed abilities they do not have, clairvoyancy has yet to be fully studied.

CONTACTING THE DEAD

To contact the spirits, mediums hold a *séance*. A group of people who wish to speak with a dead person form a circle around a table and hold hands. The medium tries to summon the presence of a spirit. Mediums have been known to fake the responses of spirits by using machines that hit the bottom of the table to produce ghostly knocks in reply to questions. However, some mediums have produced effects that cannot be explained under test conditions designed by scientists to expose them as frauds.

THE CASE OF KATIE KING

One famous medium was investigated by the Victorian scientist William Crookes. Florence Cook claimed she could summon the spirit of Katie King (*right*) who appeared at séances and talked to guests. Florence was suspected of dressing up as the spirit herself or of having someone else do so. Crookes said that his investigation had convinced him that the spirit was real. Crookes didn't publish his finding in any scientific journals but he never changed his story. Later, it was claimed that he had helped in the medium's trickery in order to have an affair with her.

QUESTIONING THE SPIRITS

It may seem strange today, but in ancient times it was common to ask spirits for advice. Oracles were people who went into a trance to ask spirits questions. They often asked the questions for other people who couldn't talk to spirits themselves. One of the most famous oracles was Pythia, the Oracle at Delphi in Greece. She used volcanic fumes to aid her visions. Ancient and modern mediums have asked many questions of the spirits and entered into long conversations with some of them. Still, no real answers have ever been given about life after death or proven that spirits exist.

FOOD FOR THOUGHT

If there is life after death, then it would make sense for dead spirits to want to contact the living. Ghosts might be trying to tell the living something important. Spirits contacted by mediums might want their family to know they are happy and at peace. Some mediums are fakes who take advantage of people who are desperate for contact with a dead loved one. In their own defense, mediums might say they are only trying to provide comfort for the grieving. And just because some are fakes doesn't prove they all are. Some could be real.

NORTH AMERICA

BERMUDA

FLORIDA

MIAMI

SAN JUAN

PUERTO RICO

MYSTERY, MYTH & PROPHECY

It is human nature to try to understand the nature of what happens around us. Until we understand unexplained events we cannot make informed choices about how to react to them. Myths usually start after something has happened that cannot be explained. As science advances, more is understood about the world and how it works. Nevertheless, many mysteries still exist. Strange events occur every day and, because it takes time to make sense of them, myths can grow. Mysteries, like our belief in psychic phenomena, are hard to figure out since they involve the nature of belief itself.

THE BERMUDA TRIANGLE

In 1945, five Avenger bomber planes took off from Fort Lauderdale, Florida. They disappeared without a trace near the Bermudas, a small group of islands in the Atlantic Ocean. The boat sent to search for them also vanished. Since then, hundreds of other ships and planes have disappeared in the same triangle of sea. Explanations have included alien abduction, sea monsters, and unusual magnetic forces. A magnetic storm could cause instruments to fail, and lost pilots could run out of fuel.

FOOD FOR THOUGHT

The law of probability says that out of a huge number of predictions, some of them are bound to come true. Those that don't are quickly forgotten. The same law can be applied to the Bermuda Triangle. In any area of 250,000 square miles, disappearances happen. The Bermuda Triangle is an area of extreme weather conditions. Probability could also be a factor in the curse of Tutankhamen. Opening a tomb sealed for over 3,000 years could release unknown bacteria. However, people like myths. Today, the Internet spreads and adds to modern myths far more quickly than has ever been possible before. If they are believable enough they will spread, whether or not there is any real evidence to support them.

THE CURSE OF TUTANKHAMEN

In 1922, the tomb of the pharaoh Tutankhamen (1336–1327 BCE) was discovered by Howard Carter, an archaeologist working for Lord Carnarvon. It is rumored that Carter destroyed writing on the wall of the tomb that read, "Death will slay with his wings whoever disturbs the Pharaoh's peace." Death did seem to follow the project. Lord Carnarvon died in 1923 at age 57. Then an archaeologist and two businessmen died after visiting the tomb. During the next 7 years, 22 more people connected with the discovery also died, many in unusual situations. However, Carter himself lived another 17 years and died at age 65.

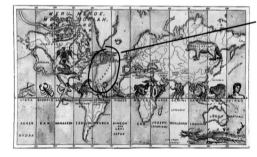

LOST BENEATH THE WAVES

The lost continent of Atlantis was said to have been the center of a highly advanced civilization. According to ancient legends, Atlantean scientists understood the human mind and were great magicians. It was said that Atlantis was destroyed by a volcanic eruption, earthquake, and tidal wave that all happened at the same time. Some people believe that some Atlanteans escaped and preserved their magical arts. No convincing evidence for Atlantis has ever been found.

TITANIC DISASTER

me disasters are
etold (predicted).
redictions can be
ten down before
event, which may
seem to prove a
erson's ability to
retell the future.

Before major
sters, such as the
ing of the *Titanic*,
he event is often
cted. Sometimes
ailed accounts of
events are given
efore the events
r. One theory is
disasters involve
nany deaths they
e an energy that
can be felt by
ensitive psychics.
This cannot be
proven, although
people who do
not consider
emselves psychic
also experience
onitions (feelings
that something is
going to happen
before it does).

NOSTRADAMUS AND PROPHECIES

Nostradamus was a French doctor known for his treatment of plague, a disease
that killed many people. In 1555, he published a book of prophecies in the form
of poems. The poems were hard to interpret. His followers believe he predicted
various important events, but his prophecies are so vague it is difficult to match
them to specific events. Some people interpreted this prophecy as foretelling the
1945 bombing of Hiroshima and Nagasaki in Japan: "Near the harbor and in two
cities will be two scourges, the like of which have never been seen. Hunger,
plague within, people thrown out by the sword will cry for help from the great
immortal God."

BOARD GAMES

Originally called the planchette, Ouija dates from the 1850s. It was a triangular board supported by two wheels and a pencil. Hands placed on the surface moved the board, and the pencil wrote messages (apparently from the spirits) on a piece of paper beneath it. In 1868, American toy companies copied the idea. They made a board with the letters of the alphabet and the words "yes" and "no." The planchette then only had to move from letter to letter to spell out its message. A Ouija board is a popular way of contacting spirits during a séance. The messages can easily be faked by players moving the planchette.

RECEPTIVE MINDS

Meditation is a method of clearing the mind. Many psychics use it to prepare their minds to receive telepathic thoughts or messages from the spirit world. Meditation is also used in prayer, in healing, and as a relaxation technique. Meditating for a long time can bring about a trance-like state in which the mind concentra entirely on a single thought. Yo is an Asian meditation technique that has become more popular in the West.

MUSIC FROM THE GRAVE

Some mediums specialize in contacting the spirits of famous people. Rosemary Brown, a London housewife, claims she has been contacted by the spirits of many famous composers. She contacted Beethoven, who told her to write down musical scores. Experts have said her work is more than just imitation. Rosemary's lack of musical training means she has only been able to record small pieces of music. Another medium, Stella Horrocks, writes whole novels that she claims have been given to her by dead authors such as Jane Austen. She goes into a trance to write. The handwriting for each writer is different.

EXORCISM

Some religions still perform exorcisms. These rituals do not summon spirits. They try to drive them away. In the Bible, exorcisms are performed to cast out demons who have *possessed* (taken over) a person's body. Nowadays, exorcism is used to get rid of ghosts or spirits. An exorcist commands the possessing spirit to leave using the name of God. Exorcism, like a powerful spell, requires three items for the ritual—a Bible, a bell, and a candle.

CONTACTING THE SUPERNATURAL

Many psychics and mediums believe the spirit world can be contacted. Some psychics believe people leave images of themselves wherever they have been. Police have hired psychics to help catch criminals. The psychics identify criminals by the image they left at a crime scene. Psychics have also been known to track down missing people, both alive and dead. Many methods are used to contact spirits, including hypnotism. The variety of methods used by psychics and mediums is one reason why scientists have found it difficult to prove or disprove their abilities.

AUTOMATIC WRITING

Writing without controlling what is written could be thought of as receiving messages from the spirit world. A person enters a trance while holding a pen or pencil. The person stares at the reflection of a candle in a mirror. The writing produced usually doesn't make sense. It is sometimes treated as if it's full of meaning. This is not generally thought of as a very believable spiritualist technique because the trance state can easily be faked.

FOOD FOR THOUGHT

These methods assume that spirits can be controlled or contacted by living people through the power of rituals. People use special items, words, music, or mental preparation to open up a link to the spirit. They might use this link to try to get rid of a spirit or to ask it for help. The ritual may be intended to affect the spirit. The medium may try to strengthen or weaken the spirit's hold on the ordinary world. Or the person contacting the spirit may be trying to raise his or herself to a "higher plane." It's easier for you to judge whether something has worked on you than it is to know whether you've affected another spirit.

TERMS USED IN DIVINATION

Astrology
Fortune-telling using the signs of the zodiac (stars).

Cartomancy
Fortune-telling with playing cards.

Catoptromancy
Using mirrors to predict the future.

Chiromancy
Reading the lines on a person's hand to see their future and character.

Geomancy
Telling the future through looking at land forms or the patterns made by dust on a flat surface.

Metascopy
Telling fortunes from lines on the forehead.

Necromancy
Gaining information from the dead.

Oneiromancy
Telling the future from dreams.

Rhabdomancy
Dowsing (using a special stick called a divining rod) to find water, treasure, or lost objects.

CROSS MY PALM WITH SILVER

Fortune-telling for money has been around for centuries. It is most often connected to the Romany or gypsy lifestyle. Traditionally, Romany families are believed to have strong psychic powers. Gypsies, who used to travel widely across Europe in caravans, were seen as good fortune-tellers. A crystal ball is often used by fortune-tellers and mediums who claim they can predict the future by looking into it.

DIVINATION

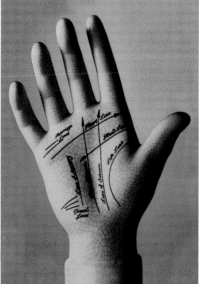

Divination means to foretell the future. It also means to reveal what is hidden by magical, mystical, or supernatural means. Many of the divining methods that have been used for centuries are still in use today. Divination often involves a set of symbols which can represent feelings, events, and personal qualities. Fortune-tellers make predictions about the future by choosing these symbols and observing which ones occur in patterns. Other forms of divination involve seeing visions of the future or making observations based on a person's physical qualities (like lines on the palm of the hand).

THE ZODIAC

The Ram, the Bull, the Heavenly Twins.
Next to the Crab, the Lion shines, the Virgin and the Scales.
The Scorpion, Archer and He-Goat,
The Man who carries the Watering Pot and the
Fish with the glittering tails.

This verse, "The Hunt of the Heavenly Host," helps us to remember the twelve astrological signs that make up the *Zodiac*. The Zodiac is a system used in several divining methods. The position of the planets, sun, moon, and signs of the Zodiac at the time a person is born is believed to define their personality. The signs are divided into four groups. Each group is matched with an element: earth, fire, air, or water. For example, Leo is a fire sign. A person who is a Leo is likely to love adventure and be driven to achieve goals.

PALM READING

Palmistry, or *chiromancy*, is a form of divination that uses the lines on the palm of a hand. Unlike Tarot, Rune-casting, and I Ching, these predictions are based on an observed quality of the person. Each line on the hand is matched with a different part of life. Definitions of the lines have developed over time. They usually include the Life Line, the Health Line, the Line of Fortune, and the Line of Fate. Breaks and bends in the various lines indicate important events in a person's life.

 **FOOD FOR THOUGHT**

Divination or guesswork? Experienced fortune-tellers can make good guesses about the future of a person simply from their personality and what they look like. Predicting romance for a pretty girl or good fortune for someone who looks rich is almost certain to be right.

CASTING THE ORACLE

Divination may be done by throwing down small objects and reading the patterns they make. In ancient times, this method of divination was called "casting the oracle" (casting means throwing). Originally, these methods were used for practical purposes, not as entertainment. The objects used were simple things that were easily found or made. Over the years, rituals developed around the forms of divination. The sets of cards, stones, and sticks used became fancier and more detailed.

FORTUNE-TELLING WITH TEA LEAVES

Reading fortunes in tea leaves is not popular now that tea usually comes in teabags. Reading tea leaves is a simple form of divination. Once the tea in a cup has been drunk, the cup is turned counterclockwise three times. The patterns the leaves form are read to predict coming events. Romany gypsies have a whole language of pictures with which to interpret the patterns. A padlock, for example, indicates a door to success is about to open.

RUNE STONES

Casting rune stones is an ancient Scandinavian form of divination. The word *runa* means mystery in Anglo-Saxon. Rune masters were tribal magicians who used the power of their hidden language to affect the weather, the harvest, healing, war, and love. The traditional Germanic set of runes uses an alphabet of three sets of eight runes. The first is called the futhark. Later alphabets contain a blank rune to represent the unknowable. As with cards used in divination, the runes are drawn face-down. They are laid down in a pattern that allows their symbolic meanings to be applied to a particular question.

DOWSING FOR WATER

Dowsing is simply *water-divining* (looking for water). Some dowsers can also find electrical cables, minerals, and oil. Some dowsing is no longer regarded as especially paranormal, and has become accepted in the modern world. Traditionally, a forked stick is held out by a dowser as he or she walks through the countryside. If water is nearby, usually under the earth, the dowsing rod twitches. It has been suggested that dowsers are particularly sensitive to the Earth's magnetic field. However, some dowsers have found water by holding a pendulum over a map.

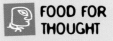
The Magician

THE TAROT

The *Tarot* is a special deck of cards used for divination. A Tarot deck doesn't use the four suits of hearts, spades, diamonds, and clubs that are in a deck of normal playing cards. Instead, the Tarot deck uses suits of cups, swords, wands, and discs. Each suit has a court card. The Tarot deck also contains 22 greater trumps (cards not in the four suits) known as the Major Arcana. All the cards have symbolic meanings as well as their stated meaning. The different Tarot decks offer different interpretations. The Magician, for example, could mean willpower or skill. During a Tarot reading the cards are laid facedown in certain positions to focus on different parts of the subject's life. They are then turned over and interpreted.

THE I CHING

The Chinese *I Ching*, or *Book of Changes*, is one of the oldest oracle books in the world. It has existed in its present form for at least 3,000 years. Divination based on the *I Ching* does not predict specific events. Instead, it shows possible outcomes of certain actions. It contains 64 hexagrams (images with six parts). Each has six lines, which are each either broken or unbroken. Using chance activities such as drawing straws or flipping a coin, a hexagram is produced and interpreted using the *I Ching*.

DREAMS & VISIONS

KUBLA KHAN'S PLEASURE DOME

In 1797, the poet Samuel Taylor Coleridge composed 300 lines of poetry while he was dreaming. When he woke up he could remember the poem and began to write it down. After being interrupted by a visitor he was unable to remember the rest of the poem. There are many examples of other writers, musicians, and artists being inspired by their dreams. Parapsychologists think that the sense of PSI (paranormal sensory information) is not as strong as the senses of touch, taste, smell, hearing, and sight. Because it is weaker, it works better when there are no distractions, such as while a person sleeps.

Scientists are still studying how the unconscious mind works. In his study of the unconscious, the father of modern psychology, Sigmund Freud (1856–1939), paid special attention to the role of dreams. A Swiss psychologist, Carl Jung (1875–1961), later suggested that everyone shared a similar unconscious in which certain images appear over and over. Each image had its own symbolism. Until the twentieth century, there was no methodical study of the human mind. Psychology (the study of the mind), like neuroscience (the study of the brain), is still a young science. Parapsychology (the study of psychic phenomena) draws on these other sciences, but there is still much to be learned.

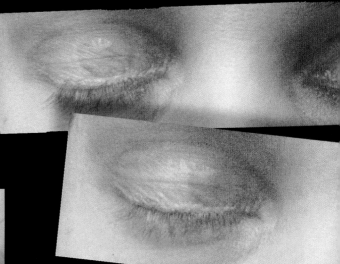

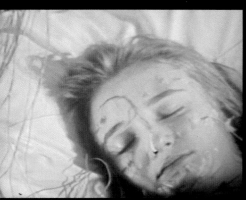

SLEEP RESEARCH

Studies conducted on sleeping people showed that they were more open to receiving psychic messages while in their REM period of sleep. Experiments involved one psychic sending images to another psychic. Both were at different stages of a sleep cycle. Woken up after each stage, the person could remember the images better after REM sleep.

REM SLEEP

The mind is active and people dream during the rapid eye movement (REM) stages of deep sleep. The body goes through five stages from deep to light sleep. During deep sleep, the body repairs itself. People dream every time they sleep. But they might not remember their dreams. A method known as lucid dreaming trains the sleeping mind to control what happens in dreams.

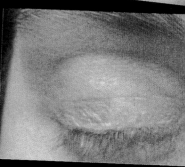

ANALYSIS OF DREAMS

There have been many theories about dreams. Ancient peoples believed they were messages from the gods. Freud, one of the first scientists who tried to explain dreaming, thought dreams were the wishes of the unconscious mind. More recently, Jung (right) wrote that in dreams people are creative and face their fears. Modern sleep research suggests that dreams are probably the result of the brain trying to store memories. Dreams are closely linked with the study of psychic phenomena because both are workings of the mind and only partly understood.

OUT-OF-BODY EXPERIENCES

Many people have reported having near-death or out-of-body experiences. They commonly describe this as seeing a bright light pulling the soul away from the body. When the person is woken up they often report having watched their own unconscious body being brought back to life. This "astral" body is claimed to be identical to the physical body, but it is transparent and shining. Ancient writings describe this phenomenon as a supernatural power that can be gained through magic or meditation. Skeptics consider it hallucination (seeing something that isn't real) or delusion (beliefs that aren't based on truth).

 **FOOD FOR THOUGHT**

Dream and vision events can be thought of as the mind behaving strangely when it is on the edge of consciousness or beyond. Some artists, such as Salvador Dali, put themselves into this state on purpose. They believed it put them in touch with a higher level of reality and produced images meant to speak directly to their unconscious. They thought these might contain universal symbols of a shared unconscious. Most people probably think their dreams would make wonderful films or books. Dreams are never easy to write down when you've woken up, though!

EXPERIMENTS OF THE MIND

TELEPATHY

Paranormal research has recorded many instances of telepathy in everyday life. Close family relationships, especially between twins, tend to make telepathic connection more likely. Some experiments in which the participants try to communicate over long distances have achieved impressive results. However, if ESP is some kind of mental radio, it is proving very difficult to tune. Despite the high success rates, experiments have yet to prove the existence of telepathic communication.

Parapsychology is the study of unusual mental phenomena, such as telepathy. These events are experienced by human beings but seem to have no physical cause. Many scientists do not trust parapsychology because it has become connected, wrongly, with other paranormal events such as alien abductions.

Parapsychology research includes studying *extrasensory perception* (ESP), which is the ability to receive information that is not available to the five senses. It also looks at *psychokinesis* (PK), which is the ability to change the state of physical objects with the mind. Out-of-body experiences are also part of parapsychology. The study of parapsychology assumes that the human mind has more power than most people believe.

PHOTOGRAPHING AURAS

Many mediums have claimed they can see an aura of light around the human body. In 1939, a Russian engineer, Semyon Kirlian, developed a method that could sense heat and electromagnetic fields to diagnose illness. He photographed these auras. His pictures showed people surrounded by a colored ring of light.

MILITARY USES OF PSI

Ever since the days when magic was used to protect the tribe, psychic phenomena have been studied as a possible military aid. During the Cold War (following World War II), the American and Russian governments studied paranormal sensory information (PSI) and how it could be used. For some years there were rumors about a secret defense project at the Pentagon, known as Operation Stargate. Some people thought the military was training psychics to use their abilities to see into enemy bases. They also thought psychics might be able to confuse foreign military leaders.

JOSEPH RHINE

In 1927, Dr Joseph Rhine an his wife, Louisa, started the first study of ESP at Duke University in North Carolina. This was the beginning of th science of parapsychology. Rhine invented the term "ESP" an spent 50 years studying it. His work was first published in 1934. Scientists immediately found fault with his laboratory techniques and statistical analysis. Rhine successfully defended his techniques, but man thought his studies must have been faked.

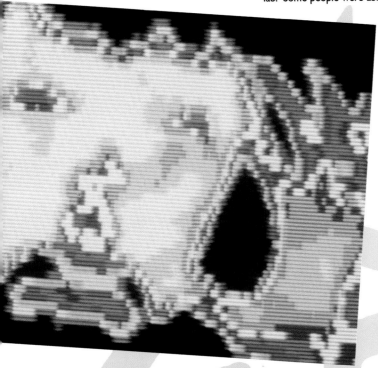

ZENER CARDS

...e of the earliest experiments in finding psychic ability were Zener cards. A deck of Zener cards contains twenty-five cards ...ided into five sets of five cards. Each card in a set had one of five different signs on it. The cards were shuffled. One at a ...e, a "sender" would try to telepathically send the sign on each card to someone across the room. That person would try to "see" which card the sender was sending. Rhine achieved a high success rate with this experiment in the lab. Some people were able to name the entire deck of cards correctly. Others could predict ahead of time what order cards would be shuffled into.

 FOOD FOR THOUGHT

There is a one in five chance of correctly guessing which Zener symbol is being "sent." If an experiment is done using 100 cards the person "receiving" is likely to guess right 20 times. Anything much above that may suggest that ESP is happening. Parapsychology research has rarely been taken seriously by mainstream science. Many doubt that the experiments work. It is difficult to design an experiment that makes it impossible for anyone to accuse the researcher of faking results. Indeed, some well-known experiments have been faked. Others were interpreted with a desired result already in mind. There is always a possibility that if a researcher is convinced that the phenomenon is real, they'll see what they want to believe.

MESMERIZING MINDS

Franz Mesmer (1734–1815) was an Austrian physician. He believed the human body had magnetic properties that could be used to cure illness. Mesmer performed public healings that involved connecting people by cords to a tub of water filled with iron filings. He achieved some successes, but most scientists did not believe his results. He was called a fraud. Although Mesmer's work is not thought to be real, it paved the way for the study of hypnotism and the unconscious mind.

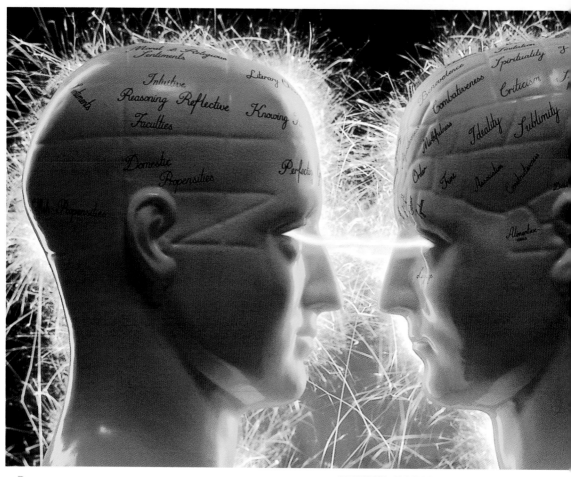

MENTAL RADIO

Recent paranormal research has been trying to understand what happens when telepathic communication takes place. It may be possible to observe brain activity during a psychic episode by recording the pattern of brainwaves of a person in an experiment. Some studies suggest there may be changes in alpha waves, the carrier signal for the working of the mind, when psychic abilities are being used.

 **FOOD FOR THOUGHT**

If people can really be trained to use ESP and telepathy, there are many practical uses for these skills. What might happen if people could read each other's minds or communicate by thought alone? It might lead to a future in which we happily live in peace. It might lead to a nightmare of a spy-state in which none of our thoughts could be private. Many researchers think that mental powers can affect mechanical systems. They now ask "What is it?" instead of "Does it exist?"

BIOGENETIC FORCE

In 1926, Russia was one of the first countries to do scientific research into psychic phenomena. Soviet scientists studied the physical conditions needed to allow the mind to send energy. In the 1970s, they studied a Russian housewife named Nina Kulagina. In a laboratory, she was able to move objects, create burn marks, and increase the magnetic properties of objects without touching them. The force Kulagina's mind appeared to have has been called *bioenergetics*.

ESP & PK

The two areas of psychic phenomena studied most are *extrasensory perception* (ESP) and *psychokinesis* (PK). ESP research generally includes *telepathy* (direct mind-to-mind communication), *precognition* (knowing about unplanned future events), and *clairvoyance* (having "second sight," or the ability to foretell future events). PK is the movement of objects with thought alone. PK may explain the apparent existence of *poltergeists*. Poltergeists are ghosts that cause objects to break, move, or float in the air. It has been suggested that a teenager, in a strong mental response to emotional problems, could cause uncontrolled PK.

GANZFELD EXPERIMENTS

The ganzfeld (total field) experiment was designed by parapsychologists to answer claims of experimental error. To reach a relaxed and ready state, people to be studied were put in a lab with nothing to see, hear, or touch. A sender then tried to telepathically communicate a randomly-selected image to the receptive person. The receiver said aloud all their thoughts. This included any images they saw or feelings they had. The ganzfeld experiment achieved a high success rate. Images were sent and received more than would be predicted by the theory of probability.

RANDOM NUMBERS, DEFINITE RESULTS

Since electronic and computer technology became widespread, parapsychologists have conducted a series of experiments on the relationships between mind, matter, and energy. One such experiment measured the human ability to affect a random event, such as the number on a number cube when it is rolled. Random number generator (RNG) machines produce a list of numbers that a person cannot change by any physical means. Experiments showed that most humans can influence which numbers will come up. The success rate seems higher when the moon is full. At full moon, magnetism in the brain may be affected by the Earth's magnetic field.

PSYCHOKINESIS

In the 1920s, Baron Albert von Schrenk-Notzing, who studied the paranormal, worked with Stanislava Tomczyk (*right*) and Willy Schneider to convince scientists and members of the English Society for Psychical Research that it was possible to levitate objects (make them float) by no known physical means. Neither the psychics nor Schrenk-Notzing were ever suspected of fraud.

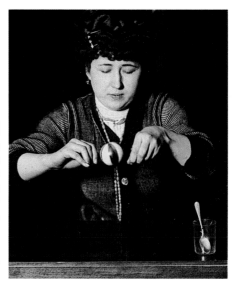

PLACES OF POWER

Despite all the research into the subject, psychic phenomena remain a mystery. We cannot say with any certainty whether or not they actually exist or how they work. However, just as our ancestors were, we are interested in psychic power and its possible uses. Over the centuries, the mystery of psychic phenomena has inspired many attempts to use these unknown powers. Those attempts left traces scattered across the world in the form of places of power. Some are natural sites in the landscape that are considered sacred. Others were built as centers for religious beliefs, magical practices, or superstitions. These ancient places are thought to symbolize psychic forces that we do not yet understand.

LINES OF POWER

Ley lines are channels of power that some people say run all over the Earth. Some people believe dowsers can control these forces to help them find water or metals. It has been suggested that ley lines may have been constructed by ancient humans or an ancient advanced civilization. They also might simply be natural features of the Earth. Large monuments or standing stones often indicate the presence of ley lines nearby. It has also been suggested that ley lines may be found by changes in radio waves. In England, ley lines are believed to cross Glastonbury Tor (*above*), a place of great religious importance.

MAGIC OF THE ANCIENTS

The pyramids at Giza are some of the oldest man-made structures in the world. They were built before 2500 BCE by Egyptian pharaohs (kings). When the pharaohs died, they were buried in the pyramids. Their bodies were mummified (preserved). The Egyptians believe that they could take their valuable possessions with them into the afterlife. Their possessions would show how rich and powerful they were. By studying the Great Pyramid, modern mathematicians have found out that ancient Egyptians understood very complicated math. They also knew the number of days the Earth takes to circle the sun and the dates of important events in the future. Recently it has been suggested that the pyramids are positioned in the same pattern as the stars in the constellation of Orion.

SACRED SITES OF THE ANCESTORS

Ayers Rock (Mount Uluru) in the Northern Territory of Australia is the largest single rock formation in the world. It is very spiritually important to the Aboriginal people. Many of the stories about Uluru are secret and are never repeated to outsiders. Many ancestral sites are around Uluru. Out of respect for Aboriginal beliefs, the Australian government has limited tourist access to the area.

STANDING STONES

Stonehenge in England was built around 1200 BCE. We do not know what its purpose was. It may have been a place to observe the stars, a Druid religious center, or a burial ground. In 1977, the Dragon Project was started to study electrical and magnetic forces around Stonehenge and other monuments. There are many other standing stone monuments in the world. Some of the most impressive are Carnac in Brittany, Msoura in Morocco, and at Lake Turkana in Kenya.

 **FOOD FOR THOUGHT**

Everyone feels a sense of wonder and mystery when at one of these places of power. You don't have to share the beliefs of the people who built them, to be amazed by the vision and hard work that went into building them. Our ancestors may have had different beliefs, but they achieved great things. One of the most valuable things to remember about the power of the mind is that our ancestors were just as smart and able to do amazing things as we are.

In Poland, a painting of the Madonna was once slashed with swords by a group of Hussites (Christian rebels) in 1430. Despite repeated attempts to repair the painting the slashes always come back.

During a laboratory experiment in psychokinesis (PK) a piece of blank paper was left in a typewriter. Scientists made sure that nobody could sit down and use it. Some time later, the paper was examined and the following unsigned verse was found.

A clever man, W.E. Cox
Made a really remarkable box
In it, we, with PK
In the usual way
Wrote, spite of bands, seals and locks.

New Zealand's rugby team, the All Blacks, performs a ritual called the haka taparahi before all their games. In the tradition of the Maori people, the energetic chant and dance is meant to bring the team good luck in the game.

Ouija is a combination of the French and German words for "Yes."

THE MAGICIAN.

In the Old Testament of the Bible, there is a story about the prophet Elisha separating his spirit from his body. In the story, he sends his spirit into the tent of a Syrian king to stop his plans to destroy the Israelites.

The most amazing story is told about a famous twentieth-century Italian priest called Padre Pio. Padre Pio was able to be in two places at the same time. One night, he apparently knocked on the door of the Archbishop of Montevideo in Uruguay to tell him that one of his priests was dying. Some time later, the Archbishop met Pio. Pio told him that he had been in Uruguay that night, although his body had never left Italy.

The Australian Skeptics group is offering $80,000 to anyone who can prove that ESP, telepathy, or telekinesis is real. The prize has been offered since 1980 and is still waiting to be won.

You can find out more about the supernatural on the Internet. Why not check out these Web sites?
www.paranormalwatch.com
www.skepdic.com
www.thesupernaturalworld.com

First published in Great Britain by ticktock Publishing Ltd. Printed in China.

ISBN-13: 978-1-59905-443-8   ISBN-10: 1-59905-443-4   eBook: 978-1-60291-769-9

15 14 13 12 11   1 2 3 4 5

Picture Credits: t = top, b = bottom, c = center, l = left, r= right, OFC = outside front cover, OBC = outside back cover, IFC = inside front cover

AKG; 3br, 2tl, 6/7b, 10cb, 12tl, 16c, 21c, 24tl, 31cr. Ann Ronan @ Image Select; 2bl, 4/5t, 8tl, 15c, 17tr. British Museum; 13t. Colorific; 12/13c. Corbis; 4/5b, 8bl, 12/13b & OBC, 18bl, 26cl, 26tl, 26/27c. e.t.archive; 6/7t. Fortean; 2c, 5tr, 6c, 6/7c, 8/9b, 10l, 10/11ct, 11bl, 14 (main pic), 14/15t, 15b, 15tr, 16b, 22bl, 22/23b, 26b, 27b, 26/27t, 28cb, 28/29c, 29br, 30tl. Gamma; IFC, 7t. Geoscience; 4bl. Image Select; 9tr, 16/17b, 18c, 25tr, 31t. Images; 18tl. Science Photo Library; 24bl, 24/25c. Telegraph Colour Library; OFC (main pic), 8c. Tony Stone; 12bl, 19tr, 18/19c, 20, 22c, 22tl, 25c, 30/31 (main). Werner Foreman; 3tr.

Every effort has been made to trace the copyright holders and we apologize in advance for any unintentional omissions. We would be pleased to insert the appropriate acknowledgement in any subsequent edition of this publication.

SADDLEBACK
EDUCATIONAL PUBLISHING